POEMS FROM THE LEFT COAST

FRAGMENTS SHORED AGAINST OUR RUIN
GODDESS POEMS
Appendix of EARLY POEMS 1971-1975

By Lucy Wilson

Copyright © 2016, Lucy Wilson

Transcendent Zero Press
www.transcendentzeropress.org

All rights reserved. No part or parts of this book may be reproduced in any format without the expressed written consent of Transcendent Zero Press, or of the author Lucy Wilson.

ISBN-13: 978-0692640067
ISBN-10: 0692640061

Library of Congress Control Number: 2016933023

Printed in the United States of America

Transcendent Zero Press
16429 El Camino Real Apt. 7
Houston, TX 77062

Cover Design by: Glynn Monroe Irby

Cover images are taken from public domain:
www.bigmapblog.com (Old L.A. Picture, back cover)
egis3.lacounty.gov (New photo of L.A.)

FIRST EDITION

POEMS FROM THE LEFT COAST

FRAGMENTS SHORED AGAINST OUR RUIN
GODDESS POEMS
Appendix of EARLY POEMS 1971-1975

By Lucy Wilson

POEMS FROM THE LEFT COAST

Table of Contents

PART ONE: FRAGMENTS SHORED AGAINST OUR RUIN / 9-46

I. RUNES OF LOVE pages 9-18

I Ching # 59 / 11

A Bankrupt Strategy / 12-13

Directions / 13

Loss / 14

Promises / 14

Substitutes / 15

Why You Must Live Longer / 15

Dear God / 16

Carpe Diem for the Kinesthetically Challenged / 17

II. LEARNING FROM NATURE pages 19-32

Flight / 21

Be Here / 21

Teaching / 22

Pain Mismanagement / 22

Pain and Yoga / 23-24

Haikus (more or less) / 25

Celebrate Impermanence / 26

Mornings in a New Place / 26

Ever / 27

Devolution / 27

A Day in the Life / 28

Awaken the Snake / 28

WARNING / 28

Poet's Burden / 29

Salute to the Sun / 29

Dolphins Do Everything Better / 30

Birds of Playa Vista / 31

Summers in Timber Trails / 32

III. SKETCHES pages 33-46

Pope Francis in Philadelphia / 35

Showdown / 36-37

Lulu / 38

At Home in the Universe / 39

Barking in the Night / 40

Cosmic Boy / 41

r/evolution / 42

To Uncle Joe, on His 88th Birthday / 43-44

Doll's Song / 44

March of the Trolls / 45

PART TWO: GODDESS POEMS / 47-72

Welcome / 49

Introduction: Bring Back the Goddess / 50-51

Goddess Litany / 52

Demeter / 53-54

Lilith / 55

Eve Would Like to Have a Word / 56

Daughter of the Swan / 57-58

Circe's Story / 59-60

Goddess of Love / 61-62

Mary Speaks / 62

The Magdalene / 63-64

Psyche's Prayer / 64

Hecate: Invocation of the Goddess / 65

Love Song from Sheba to Her Solomon / 66

Agamemnon and Iphigeneia / 67

Sacrificial Daughters / 68

Orpheus and Eurydice / 69-70

Orpheus / 70

Haiku: Eurydice / 71

APPENDIX: EARLY POEMS 1971-1975 / 73-87

Van Gogh / 75

Portrait of Mrs. Chagall, no. 2 / 75

Vanishing Point / 76

Nocturne / 76

Solitude / 77

Song / 78-79

Aberration / 79

The Fire / 80-81

Memory / 81

Fragments: Unrequited Love / 82

Wailing for Her Demon Lover / 83

After the First Death / 84

Vermont Holiday / 85

Untitled / 86

ABOUT THE AUTHOR / 89

Part One: Fragments Shored Against Our Ruin
I. RUNES OF LOVE

I Ching # 59

Disintegration is the path to unification.
Wind and water
cannot merge
but each intact,
its essential nature preserved,
joins with the other
in storm-force gusts.

As it was that raw day in May
in southern France,
when we roamed the seafront in San Raphael
in search of an early dinner,
blown from shops to street to restaurant
pour les moules et le vin rouge.
Revived, we braved the elements
once more. Sea and sand
and wind and man: yes, even you
looked French that day.

A Bankrupt Strategy

Religious hatred is the worst.
It feeds on choice cuts
of the human heart.
Religious hatred leaves its host
incapable of feeling the pain of others,
a short leap to inflicting pain on others that ends
with a young mother dead,
her husband dead,
fourteen of their victims dead,
a six-month infant orphaned,
and a nation in shock.

How can this happen in my place of work,
my ballpark, favorite restaurant, airport...?
Why do they hate us?
We do not dare to answer that question
for fear of looking soft on terrorism.

Violence is not the answer.
Violence is a bankrupt strategy
and a worse ideology.
Violence in the service of God
will be the downfall of the human race.

Who will speak for the children,
heirs of our errors?
We must keep our enemies closer
even than our friends.
We must listen to young people
who are so passionate
about everything.

We must resist the urge
to stigmatize a complex mixture
of cultures and ethnicities
that have little in common
except their Muslim faith.
When hate-mongers spew their venom,
look away. Do not honor them with your attention.

I say aloud: the time for cooperation is now.
Love me or hate me, but please talk to me!
Share with me your fears and dreams.

What can we do to facilitate
our fragile coexistence?
Where do we agree?
What can we do to enable dialogue?
How can we find courage and strength to compromise,
to make the future a place where
our children can live without fear
in cordial multiplicity and mutual respect?

Directions

Is this a love poem
a how-to manual
online instructions
GPS directions
or a dog-eared map?
It matters not
as long as it gets me
from where I am
to where you are
waiting for me.

Loss

Each day she mourns me
though I am never far.
She is learning to hear my voice
in the cheeping, peeping, burbling sound
of morning in the desert,
and in the humming roar of cicadas any time,
day or night.

Promises

Take my hand, love, and lead the way to a better place.
I'm tired of living on ashes and dust,
on mold spores and rust,
on wishes and dreams,
on hopes and schemes.
I'd rather eat cat food or rat food or kale,
just don't make promises that are doomed to fail.

Substitutes

I asked for lobster
and got jumbo shrimp.
I called for wine
and got grape juice.
Filet mignon turned out to be ground beef.
Olive oil ... bacon fat
silk scarf ... polyester
Baroque quartet ... commercial jingle
epic tale ... soap opera
hand woven ... mass produced.
Shall I go on?

Why You Must Live Longer

Who will lecture me
 on matters of race and power
 late at night when sensible people are asleep?

Who will correct my grammar
 (*my* grammar!) and explain rhetorical strategies?

Who will urge me to watch Al Jazeera and BBC
 instead of CNN and MSNBC?

Who will remind me that nearly everything
 wrong with this country
 has roots in slavery?

Who will protect me from those who wish
 to see me fail?

Who straddles worlds
 and code switches with ease?
Who cooks and plays piano,
 alto and soprano sax — baseball too?

Who prefers his own company
 or that of his dog?

Who knows me as well as I know myself?
Who keeps me honest,
 shares my pain,
 holds my well-being in the palm of his hand?

Dear God,

Please don't take Roland now:
it's really not a good time.
He has children who need him
and friends who love him.
Enemies too, but the worst
and most powerful
is the one he sees in the mirror
when he shaves. He loves that face
and hates it too. The history of the world
is written in that face.

Yours sincerely,
Lucy

Carpe Diem for the Kinesthetically Challenged

After seven weeks recovering from foot surgery,
yoga is like being born again into a world
so familiar but more fragile, ephemeral,
fraught with unexpected joy and pain.

Envy the palm trees, celebrating every gust
of wind by waving palm fronds at the clear blue sky,
begging her to join their dance.
Seven weeks, long enough: I must move or go mad.

Come on, Roland, let's raise Cain;
age and illness will win the game,
but we'll give them a run for their money.
We'll sit on the porch swing when it's warm and sunny,
and laugh at jokes that only we find funny.

Part One: Fragments Shored Against Our Ruin
II. LEARNING FROM NATURE

Flight

"Love never hurt a winged creature."
　　　Anon 1100 BC

　　1
Do birds in flight
carry their loved ones
in their hearts?

　　2
If I could fly I'd not come down
except to eat and sleep.
I'd dance among the treetops, high
above this wicked world.

Be Here

Yoga is conscious living.
Tougher than it sounds.
Count breaths,
listen to your body,
any and all bodies,
all of life.
You are one with all:
all one
all you.

Teaching

As the sun rises
my west facing windows
glow in reflected light.

Teaching is reflected light.
My teachers touch my students' lives
though they will never meet.
Transference. Transformation.
In what unfamiliar faces
will my light shine?

Pain Mismanagement

Curled on yoga mat
I'm hiding from pain,
my persistent friend.
Perhaps illness is an honor,
brevity of life
preferable to longevity.
Perhaps the point is
to move on.

Pain and Yoga

Not a question of why
or a matter of lamenting loss
of flexibility, mobility, beauty, memory.
Alas, memories of youthful abilities
can hurt more than help:
gymnastics in high school,
summer swim competitions,
horseback riding as a child and young adult,
riding my bike from West Philadelphia to Temple
during halcyon grad school days,
amazing my friends by standing on my head
with legs in full lotus position.
Yoga came naturally, easily,
enhancing my flexibility
and giving me the key to future pain and immobility.

Parkinson's disease.
At forty-eight my world collapsed
when the handsome doctor cheerfully confirmed
my deepest fears. Like a deer in headlights
I could not move or breathe
at the realization that my life
as I had known it was over.

Reanimation. The deer blinks, shivers, and leaps
to safety in the nick of time.
Picture this:
You can't move, can hardly breathe
as painful spasms roll across your chest and back,
like waves on a rough sea, relentlessly, increasingly powerful.
 And then you remember:
breathe deeply, clear your mind, sit comfortably and relax.
Look around for hand-holds in the sheer cliffs
of gall and granite. Breathe as deeply as your pain will permit.

Bend backwards across the bed, relaxing one vertebra
at a time. No fast moves! We are tip-toeing past
the sleeping giant, Pain, in our quest for reanimation,
resurrection, return to the soothing darkness
that is the Great Spirit's cooling breath:
alpine winds
lake breezes
ceiling fans on hot days
soothing sounds of nightfall
birds' calls
lake water lapping at the shore
a window open to the spring rain.

Thus endeth the lesson.
Apply as needed.

Haikus (more or less)

Another day
in Los Angeles:
sun and more sun.

On her throne
Katie Kuwaiti Kat
surveys all.

Let go.
Don't look back.
I'm here.

Self-sustaining fire,
coiled snake:
unleash the power within.

Look for me
on the embarcadero:
be discreet.

Flights canceled due to
a high wind from Jamaica
heading toward L.A.

Celebrate Impermanence

Permanence is boring,
no room for dreams.
Change enables the dreamers
who send pictures from the front.

Mornings in a New Place
(Playa Vista)

Different birds sing here
such as the early morning dove
complaining to the dawn
about so many things
in that mournful cry,
or is that me?
Pathetic fallacy:
The world is not an echo
of my sad song.

Ever

Can we return to an aquatic state?
Can we will ourselves to fly?
If you can dream it, it's been dreamed,
if you can sing it, it's been sung,
if you can feel it
then there's someone out there feeling it too.
Just don't ask for anything forever,
for "ever" is a long, long time.

Devolution

Return to an aquatic state:
vestigial gills
scales for skin
swimming through mountain passes
long hidden from view.
Breathing is so retro!

A Day in the Life

Coerced, compelled, constructed and undone,
impaled, ignored, forgotten, on the run,
panic, nausea, night sweats and the rest:
another day of living, not the worst, not the best.

Awaken the Snake

Coiled in the belly
content and warm:
dare we waken the sleeping reptile?
Can you feel it moving upward
through the gates of the city
till your walls fall
revealing the light being
beneath the skin?

WARNING

Life is dangerous to your mental health
and the body doesn't fare too well either.

Poet's Burden

Poets don't have the luxury
of waiting for humanity's perfection.
It's up to us to make it happen,
to share ourselves,
to live consciously,
to embrace death,
to celebrate ephemerality
to remind the evolutionarily challenged
that we have all the answers inside ourselves:
the trick is asking the right questions.

Salute to the Sun

The morning sun
washes the world,
dew drops anoint us,
and palm fronds
wave benediction
as we witness the return
of color, size, texture, contrast.

Darkness before and after:
celebrate light!

Dolphins Do Everything Better

Given the choice, would you wear clothes?
Clothing binds and bags and slows us down:
we bipeds have barely left the gate when this majestic creature
has reached the perimeter by leaps and bounds,
returned to the starting point and dashed off again,
ever on the lookout for further opportunities to sport and play.

We're confined to land and they to sea
but our ships and sewage plants encroach
on their territory. They do not retaliate.
They remain on the ocean side of existence,
singing like Tibetan meditation bowls, as they glide
effortlessly through the sea.

One glimpse of these aquatic mammals
shores up our flagging enthusiasm for life and love.
Dolphins are the true sages,
a point of intersection
between water and air, self and soul, human and divine.
We lose them and we lose our souls.

Dolphins make days brighter
nights safer
joys less transitory
sorrows swift
pain purposeful.
Without dolphins, we have nothing.

The Birds of Playa Vista

The rooster starts crowing before the sun has risen,
before the sky begins to shed its cloak of darkness,
before the morning fog lifts or other birds add their voices
to the chorus. In spring the cock was followed
by Canadian geese flying overhead, stopping in California —
snow birds returning from warmer climates but not
in a hurry to continue their journey home.
By July the geese have departed, taking their young with them,
calling to their fellow travelers in that nuanced bird talk
many call honking. With the geese gone, the doves join in
with their mournful sounding moan,
the sparrows add their voices,
and after that I cannot tell one songbird from another.

But I've seen the Western cardinal in his scarlet robe,
attended by his more subdued consort.
The crows' cacophony and the mocking birds' sharp tones
allow them to compete with planes landing at LAX and
the steady roar of cars racing along Lincoln Boulevard.
I'm waiting for nightfall when the crickets' chirp
and cicadas' song are drowned out
by the voices of frogs in Ballona Creek.
They are still living there, despite the drought that has
dried up the creek bed in the optimistically named Wetlands.

The frogs remain despite pollution and over-development
all around this final remnant of protected wildlife
in Los Angeles county.
Where else can the frogs go?

Summer in Timber Trails

If my body is a simple vessel,
a wooden rowboat or aluminum canoe,
then the boat that is my body
has drifted, oars up,
through shimmering late summer heat,
to the eastern end of the lake.

I lounge on rough wood seat in need of paint,
my long hair trailing in the water,
and dream of lives to come.
Dragonflies hover above my head
while lily pads, like paving stones,
lead deep into the marshland.

Golden sunlight cascades through
green woods surrounding Valley Lake.
In memory, as in an old faded photo,
my sixteen-year-old self, that August day,
became one with wooden rowboat,
with lapping lake and loons' call,
with steady hum of bees
and herons' flapping wings.

Part One: Fragments Shored Against Our Ruin
III. SKETCHES

Pope Francis in Philadelphia

Philadelphia, on a warm Indian summer day,
prepares for the visit of Pope Francis.
Why Philly, some might ask, but not those of us
who know this wonderfully diverse city,
home to African Americans, Italian Americans,
and many other hyphenated citizens
from around the world.

In downtown Philadelphia on a balmy evening,
tables and chairs wander out of restaurants and
on to the sidewalks to create a little Paris in Center City.
This is not the Paris of austere facades and
floor-to-ceiling French doors but rather a colonial town
of red brick structures glowing in the setting sun.

On CNN the talking heads describe the Pontiff's
earlier speech to Congress
as gospel-based criticism of American society.
This is a different kind of pope:
a pope who speaks his mind,
encourages participation,
demands peace, tolerance, respect.

Memorable moments:
Babies held in the Pontiff's capable hands.
Nuns grooving to the sounds of the Sledge sisters.
A nation in love with a modest, compassionate man of God.

Showdown

With his 38 caliber pistol, loaded, half hidden in his lap,
Eagle Man waits, watching the door.
The Sioux warrior is about to meet his enemy face to face.
Eagle Man has spent a lifetime battling the forces of evil
in Blue Man's vast empire,
a cursed place where greed rules
and goodness is seen as subversive
by flag-waving, gun-toting, Bible quoting, gay bashing,
women oppressing, environment trashing members
of Blue Man's private army of personal enrichment seekers.

Blue Man arrives. He has heard about this cantankerous Oglala
for whom cooperation and accommodation
are simply not options.
Since young Black Elk saw Blue Man in a vision decades ago,*
the king of greed has turned the continent
into a vast concrete slab
while species die and children cry when forced
into Wahshichu's boarding schools
where they are rewarded for conforming to alien beliefs.

Eagle Man speaks:
"State your case Blue Man, so all will know the depths
 of your depravity. What are your plans for planet earth?"

"I have three goals," replies Blue Man:
"to eradicate the Indigenous people and erase all mention
 in textbooks and museums;

"to eliminate with their demise all hope
 that Wahshichu** will learn, from Great Spirit,
 how to live in harmony with Nature;

to ensure that the Blue Plague spreads from sea to shining sea,
leaving garden planet earth as barren as the lifeless moon."

Eagle Man reflects with anger on the planet's plight,
the work of unfettered capitalists,
oil industry executives from Houston to Hermosa Beach,
practitioners of fracking and unsound farming methods,
like growers of water-guzzling monsoon crops
in the deserts of California.

Face to face for the first and last time,
Eagle Man and Blue Man feel the ground shake
from depleted aquifers and fracking.
So much of earth's substance has been harvested for profit
that earth's infrastructure is compromised.
Mountains slide into the sea, skyscrapers sway and dance
before crumbling into vast chasms,
and smaller fissures gobble up cars and trains.
Chaos reigns and Eagle Man exclaims:
"You'll never frack on this planet again, Blue Man."
As Blue Man slides toward a gaping hole in the earth's surface
he hears a thunderous flapping of wings and sees —

the last thing he'll ever see —
a great golden eagle soaring into the sky.

* See John G. Neihardt, *Black Elk Speaks* (Lincoln and London:
U of Nebraska P, 2014.

** White race.

Lulu

Your beauty and your talent
like sunlight and glacial ice
are gifts from the Universe,
a once-in-a-lifetime opportunity
available only to you.

Don't deny us the joy that you provide
with every delicate brushstroke.
Your paintings show us
the meaning of beauty. In them I see
hope for humanity.
Any species that can conceive
such delicate balance of truth and color
must be redeemable.

Your body too must be treated with love
and respect: fed, clothed, kept warm in winter.
Neglect of the body is neglect of the soul.
Higher consciousness does not have to hurt.

At Home in the Universe
   (For Brian Swimme)

Dashing figure, gentle soul:
the camera loves him
because he loves his audience.
They come from New York and North Dakota,
Szechwan and Sligo.
They call themselves Catholic and Muslim,
Jainist and Jewish, Taoist and Gnostic,
Lutheran and Libertarian.
They come to hear Brian talk about
a universe that defines us
just as we define it.
*We are the universe.**
With his comrades arm-in-arm,
eco-warriors Brian, Mary Evelyn and John
must work to heal this once great planet
mortally damaged though it well may be.

Scientist, actor, professor, and high priest:
Brian has as many roles as the day has moods
while the sun moves farther from the east
toward the birthplace of tomorrow.
Return to the source, says the old book.**
Returning to the source is serenity.
No longer alone in the universe.
Home at last in the universe.

* *Journey of the Universe*, Brian Swimme and Mary Evelyn Tucker
(New Haven: Yale University Press, 2011)

** *Tao Te Ching*

Barking in the Night

I heard coyotes
in the middle of last night,
transiting the golf course
in search of prey.
Perhaps the drought has
driven them out into the open,
or perhaps they thought
they'd beat the heat
with a 4 a.m. tee-time.
The pool man, who remembers me
from year to year,
does not fear the occasional coyote,
but he's wary when they travel in packs.

Cosmic Boy (D. D. P.)

Mild mannered visitor from another dimension,
you find yourself surrounded by homo sapiens,
dangerous because we are so violent,
contentious, insecure, insincere, unevolved.
What did you expect, a welcoming committee?
In our eyes, you are the invader, the enemy.
You arrive on the scene late in the game. Ignorance
has triumphed, meanness rules, pettiness
prevails. No sense of community, empathetically
challenged, a world of hate-filled engines
of self-destruction.

       Does life exist on other planets?
Wrong question! Are we alone here? Or do we share
this life-supporting environment with invisible presences
and alternate realities? Are you, Cosmic Boy,
an angel or a nightmare? Should we fear you
or welcome you as savior?

       Meanwhile, we'll keep you under surveillance:
you have radical change written all over your face.
The powers-that-be fear your vision, your vocabulary.

But imagine life here on earth when humans reach 10 billion.
You can fly above the fray, like a hummingbird at play,
but we humans will be tied by gravity to this wretched locality.

r/evolution

Somebody tell Cosmic Boy
about the interrelatedness of all life forms.
Assure him he is not alone.
The roulette wheel of life
is poised to start another revolution.
Seekers ride roughshod over crucial landmarks
then wonder why they've lost their way.

Remember where you came from.
Imprint on memory past victories and defeats.
Reach down deep into your soul
where nurturing earth goddess awaits your arrival.
She will cure you of you.

To Uncle Joe, on his 88th Birthday

You were present at the big events of my youth:
birthdays, weddings (elopements) and funerals.
A formal family photo taken on Nana's 75th
shows you hunkered down in a far corner of the picture,
praying for release from all this family life.

But family life is your strength. In Mary Jane
you found the perfect wife, your soulmate.
Children come and go, but Mary Jane has your back:
always! You were the great heart surgeon,
a man of means, father to nine children,
an artist in the operating room
implanting heart valves and pacemakers,
or off hours wielding paintbrush rather than scalpel,
depicting landscapes and seascapes and flowers.
Or carving wooden ducks and loons, catching record fish,
trimming bonsai and coaxing orchids into bloom.

We must have some of the same memories:
Papa's office in the house on Hollis Avenue, the sound of buses
at all hours. Papa's rose bushes in Huntington
and Nana's wall of blue hydrangeas, the goldfish pond
before it was filled in with ivy, the Webels' house,
the shady lane to the beach.

You can be scary, but your bark is worse than your bite.
You came of age when men were cool under pressure
and tough — Bogie, Tracey, Wayne —
while women stood behind their men
and felt safe. Try as you might to pass for a redneck,

a little to the right of Attila the Hun,
your quick wit and kind eyes tell another story.

You are my only uncle, sort of a surrogate dad,
and Mary Jane is my only aunt.
I think I chose well.

Doll's Song
(A response to Offenbach's "Tales of Hoffman")

Wind me up like Hoffman's doll,
a bit stiff but amazing to see:
a mechanical girl who sings
like a bird in flight.
Hands and feet in sync
while voice soars in the upper registers —
crystal smashing notes so high
lost falcons find their way home.

March of the Trolls

During death,
which starts at birth,
matter tends toward
immateriality.
Like a rotting apple
solid becomes liquid
until there is
no body left.
Your essence has moved on
to the next story
unless you have outlived
your need for narrative.

What role has suffering
in this transformation?
Is pain a test of our strength
or punishment for earthly malfeasance?
Does pain purify or punish?
Focus or limit?
Embolden or embalm?

In our beginning is our end.
Begin again?
Not if one has paid her dues:
cultivated compassion,
emerged from anger and spite,
subdued unruly passion,
found her way to the peaceful valley
on the other side of pain and fear.

Part Two: Goddess Poems

Welcome

Come in out of the cold
but leave your weapons by the door
along with hatred, fear, envy,
old grudges and new pain.
Come in under the shelter of my rainbow umbrella,
last refuge of a world gone mad.

Some call it evolution,
others revolution.
Which side are you on?
Where does difference end?
Let us pray that humankind
moves forward toward clarity
and is not held back by entrenched disunity.

Bring Back the Goddess*

When women ruled
 there was no word for war.
Where is the Goddess when we really need her?
Search the universe for the usual suspects:
Lilith and Eve,
Helen and Aphrodite,
Mother Mary and Mother Nature.
Goddess has been called many names
on her downward slide from deity to demon:
feckless, faithless, frail
menstrual, menopausal, maudlin
weak , willful, wily — in a word,
WOMAN.

We need the wisdom of ages,
 stories that tell the other side.
Industrial Revolution
becomes oil spills and air pollution.
Christ weeps when his name is used to justify
slaughter and enslavement.
The best minds in the solar system make weapons of terror
while schools deteriorate, prisons prosper,
and children die before they have lived.

It's our turn now, ladies.
We are taking back the planet.
We would have the goddess
 restored to her rightful place.
What if the rough beast's time is now,
 and we are it?
Not anarchists or terrorists or atheists:
just women!

Should we care that Adam rejected his first wife Lilith
because she tired of taking it lying down?
Is it fair that Eve gets blamed for, well, everything?
Helen remind us of the cost of beauty,
while Mothers Mary and Nature pay a cruel price
for their ties to humankind.

Join us! Volunteers needed for a grassroots campaign to
Bring Back the Goddess.
Bring Back the Eternal Feminine.
Men and donations welcome.

* Most details regarding the goddesses' lives are from *Encyclopedia of Greco-Roman Mythology* by Mike Dixon-Kennedy (Santa Barbara: ABC-CLIO, 1998).

Goddess Litany

*The Tao is older than God.**

I am the voice of ages
mother of creation
queen of the universe
nature's high priestess
alpha and omega
voice of reason
heart of justice
soul of compassion
dancer at daybreak
beloved of gods
protector of the weak
leader of the strong
healer of the sick
wisdom's domain
the lotus in the pool
love's ultima thule:
I am the Eternal Feminine.

*Lao Tzu, *Tao Te Ching*

Demeter*

Your sorrow touches my heart.
Your pain binds me to this suffering planet.
Your confusion and frustration
turn to anger in my soul.

Can you feel the weight lifting?
I am stronger than I look.
Feel freedom from heartache.
Unearth the roots of your wretchedness
and plunge them deep into my being
where they will struggle in my unfamiliar soil —
transforming dirt,
enriching mulch —
and emerge purged, pure, purring with potential.

I am Demeter, goddess of the fertile earth,
healer, helper, happy to be of use.
For this I was made.
Let me lift you up,
Wind under your wings,
suspended between sky and sea
like the Goodyear Blimp
or a red-tailed hawk,
sun streaming through her hovering form.

You are not alone,
you are loved, but first
you must embrace yourself.
The journey starts when you say yes to pain, fear, loss,
to life's brevity and love's perfidy.

Say yes to your monsters then send them all to me:
I'll teach them manners
while you run free.

* "Demeter" appeared as "Ceres" in my book of poems, *Wind on Water* (2015). It appears here with permission of the editor/publisher Transcendent Zero Press.

Lilith*

As Adam's first wife: why am I not in the Bible?
"Male and female he created them": that is me.
So I did make a brief, anonymous appearance
before getting kicked downstairs
and demoted to demon.
Barred from the Bible, I became the stuff of nightmares,
sucking life out of sleeping babes
who should have been my children.

Tales told by winners leave much unsaid.
Monolithic cultures breed enmity and the urge
to make the world in their own image,
a place of sorrow and fear.
Why, when not forgotten,
am I so loathed and disrespected?
I demand only this: that I own myself.
I belong to no man, no church, no nation.
I belong to one race: human.
I abide by just laws
and carry my weight on the journey home,
but I belong to no man, no church, no nation.
I have one job to do, to educate,
to spread knowledge of our shared humanity,
to dwell in the depths of darkness,
source of serenity.

* "Lilith" appeared in *Wind on Water* and is reprinted here with permission of editor/publisher Transcendent Zero Press.

Eve Would Like to Have a Word

Mother of the human race?
Puh-leeze!
That's like taking credit
for measles or bunions,
mosquitoes, mold.

That pernicious species homo sapiens
has much to answer for.
They don't improve with age or learn
from their mistakes.
Greed and selfishness rule
not empathy, sympathy, kindness, love.

To what extent am I to blame
for my offspring's perfidy?
I wash my hands of them.
I am sitting Shiva. Henceforth,
their names will not be spoken
except in the past tense.
I have no children.
Unmothered, humans are a sorry lot.

Daughter of the Swan

Hello! Helen here — too hot to handle —
nobody else can hold a candle
to my beauty and charm.
Oh, I've done so much harm!
Some women wreck homes:
I brought down a nation.
For my part in this tragic tale
of lust and fornication,
I present this testimony
to sacred matrimony.

Good looks are envied, but take it from me
there are way better gifts than physical beauty.
I'm not talking silky hair and young-looking skin,
I'm saying breath-taking, heart-breaking,
crazy-making occasions of sin!
Like winds that whip up desert sands
then drive through mountain passes
leaving havoc in the their wake,
a beautiful woman leaves a trail
of broken dreams and sad mistakes.

This is beauty such as gods have in their DNA
and pass on to their offspring as Zeus did me.
My poor mother, lovely Leda, never
stood a chance once the Swan decided
he would have her with or without consent.

So here I stand, a product of divine lust
and human frailty, for Leda was a helpless pawn
as soon forgotten as a dream at dawn.
My sister Clytemnestra and I would laugh
at how my appearance turned men into pigs.
Our laughter stopped when young Paris took off
with me in his luggage. Abduction or seduction?

I can hardly recall, but that event
unleashed ten years of war,
caused untold suffering,
cost countless lives,
and left a once-great city in ruins.

Murder and mayhem, rape and infidelity:
these are rewards of excessive beauty.
If you love your daughters, wish them kindness and joy,
empathy and wisdom, a sense of wonder and awe.
But most of all a heart that's steady and true.
If they are easy on the eyes, so much better for you.

Circe's Story

Some call me witch, others wise woman:
I guess it depends on your point of view.
What do you see when you look at me?
Medical knowledge or sorcery?
Healing herbs or quackery?
Fear of smart women ought to have
a Latin name like *carpe diem*
so pervasive it has come to be.
But allow me to tell my side of the story.

Daughter of deities, I grew up in privilege,
encouraged to study books and nature.
I recognized hypocrisy before I could spell it.
I still see with the child's clear, unflinching gaze
and speak my mind on matters great and small.
I am sought out by the ill, the angry, the lonely,
and by lost souls suffering from non-specific
existential malaise that takes root in consciousness
and poisons the source of our existence.

We still need to discuss the love of my life, Odysseus,
who found his way to my island home on
his journey back from Troy
to wife and son and palace.
Of course Penelope loved him,
but for twenty years she did not know
if he was even alive.
I too bore him a child (in some versions three)
though my son Telegonus became the unwitting cause
of his father's demise.

When Odysseus first saw me,
I was young and powerful,
agelessly beautiful,
healer and counselor,
scholar and practitioner:
a wise woman,
avatar to the Obeah women of Jamaica
and midwives everywhere.
My so-called "magic" had transformed the island.
I reigned in a small universe
based on truth and courage.
If I turned Odysseus's men into swine,
believe me, it was an improvement.
Ten years of war and another ten spent wandering,
they had indulged their base desires in every port
and by now were unfit for society of the better sort.

Comedies traditionally end with a wedding:
my story ends with two.
When Telegonus realized his fatal error
that ended the life of the father he was seeking,
he tried to make amends to Penelope and Telemachus,
providing them safe haven and thus to stop their weeping.
Telegonus then took Penelope for his bride
and married me to her son for our mutual safe keeping.
Though the father eluded me during his life,
I bloomed again in middle age
by agreeing to be Telemachus's wife.

Once more, I ask: what do you see
when you look at me?
Transformational knowledge or sorcery?
Medicinal herbs or highway robbery?
Comfort and advice or debauchery?
Dr. Johnson judged a society by its treatment of the poor,
but its treatment of women says even more.

Goddess of Love

Sisters, mothers, virgins, whores,
women who write, who dance,
who run corporations and countries,
school teachers and professors,
nuns, nurses and nannies:
come to me, heed my words.
I am Aphrodite, goddess of love and fertility,
beloved by gods and mortal men as well.
My many children populate mythic discourse.
Fertility cults, sacred prostitutes,
renewable virginity, worship of beauty:
if erotic love is present, so am I.

Troy was *my* project,
Helen the bait.
Promised power and fame
by Hera and Athena,
Paris took my lure —
hook, line and sinker —
when I promised him the love
of the world's most beautiful woman.
But he quickly learned, *Be careful what you wish for.*

Have you loved someone so much you felt
your heart would burst?
Have you ever risked all for love?
Does your beloved's face obscure the sun and moon?
If you answered "yes" to any of these questions,
then you are one of us.

Go to your beloved,
kiss him gently while you circle his neck with your arms.
Pull him toward you.
There is nothing and no one between you.
You are one person.

Alas, our bodies wear out
and our spirits move on,
but for this precious moment
let our love be like a cloud of pine-scented mist
that permeates our branches,
for the duration of love's day.
As you climb the steps toward the summit
recall our time together and stand tall,
for you have the look of someone who is cherished
by someone like me.

Mary Speaks

Do I mind that some dusty old medieval monk
crossed out "Queen of Heaven" and wrote
"Mother of God" in its place?
I am proud of both roles,
care little for titles,
find comfort in anonymity,
prefer the company of ordinary people
to that of gods.

But I must rouse myself,
heed the call:
my daughters need me
and my ties to deity.

So I'll return in a blaze of light
and show the skeptics my power and might,
I'll teach the ancient wisdom of the night,
the Eternal Feminine that sets all things right.

The Magdalene

If there's a Christ
then there must be
a temptress,
a tart,
a slut.
That's my part in the sacred story,
and he who wrote the story got to choose:
virgin or whore?
man or God?
glory or defeat?
He who wrote the story got to knead
soft sand into malleable clay.

What gets left out of the story is
that Jesus loved me,
made me his confidante,
charged me with his mother's care
should he be called away,
told me his secrets,
turned to me in trouble and joy.

Some say I was first among apostles,
mother of his children,
wife. . . .
Idle speculation, I say.

I know what I know:
how he trembled with rage at injustice,
how he felt others' pain and suffering
as if it were his own,
how little children followed him around,
including him in their games,
so young at heart he was.
Often I wondered if he wore himself out.

He may have been divine,
but he was all too human and very much a man.

Psyche's Prayer

Hecate, great goddess, older than time,
please help me in my hour of greatest need.
You helped Demeter find Persephone
when Hades stole the girl to be his queen.
I too am caught between a lover's arms
and a mother's love (though not for me).
Her much loved son Eros has had the nerve
to ask me, a mortal, to be his bride
while elevating me to goddess-hood —
but that enraged his mother even more.

Mother Hecate, who better than you
to assuage Aphrodite's greatest fear
that my beauty is superior to hers?
She rose from sea foam on a scallop shell
and stepped upon the shore without a stitch.
Her beauty filled the world with hope for love,
but now she doubts her power to bewitch.
She tortures me with tasks impossible
then sits and waits for me to fail,
but her plan backfired when many other gods
took pity on and helped me to succeed.

Friend to witches, dogs, and men of wealth,
your pre-Helenic origin is proof
that your wisdom springs from Eurasian roots.
But now you make your home among the dead,
inspiring living beings with awe and dread.
Unleash your powers to give me peace and calm
with my beloved Eros and his mom.

Hecate: Invocation of the Goddess

Darkness becomes Hecate, goddess most mysterious.
Some call her Zeus's daughter, but she is older than Zeus,
older than time itself.

Hear us, Hecate, be our guide,
protect us in times of strife.
Heal us, Hecate, give us what we need to survive this life.
Speak to us Hecate,
share your wisdom of the night,
show your mystical delight
In detachment from things corporeal.

Goddess in three persons,
why this loitering in graveyards and at crossroads,
where uneasy souls wander all night?
"Neither flesh nor fleshless,"*
but somewhere in between
where life sprang from nothing and to which it will return.

Still point, star balance, moments of pure being:
intimations of other dimensions
not encumbered with time and space.
Your true name cannot be spoken.
You are the final test,
the last bequest,
one's personal best,
eternal rest.

Before there was light, there was darkness.
Before there was differentiated consciousness,
there was unity of being.
Before there was God, there was Hecate.

* T. S. Eliot, "Burnt Norton"

Love Song from Sheba to Her Solomon

When at last I take my place beside you
the obstacles will disappear.
Nation, language, age, culture,
politics, religion, race, taste,
pastimes and past lives:
nothing will come between us.

So far apart, we thought we were alone
until that mid-air collision, one hot summer night,
when we tumbled each into the other's life,
igniting a fireworks display
that turned night into transcendent day.

But that was only half the battle.
We still had mountains to climb,
 dragons to slay, oceans to navigate.
We had to endure loss, feel others' pain,
win graciously, reflect on failure,
fear no evil, never look back,
 dance with the devil 'till the sun comes up.

Nights are long but life is longer.
When at last I take my place beside you
we'll sleep the dreamless sleep
in darkness both refining and renewing.
We shall save the universe
 one kiss, one gasp, one deep breath at a time.

Agamemnon and Iphigenia

What kind of goddess
would ask a father
to sacrifice his daughter
in exchange for victory in battle?
What kind of father
would comply?
When fathers use the weight of their authority
against their offspring,
daughters often disappear from view,
go underground,
move far away.

Even when they occupy the same space,
fathers and daughters do not necessarily
inhabit the same place.
Daughters live with one foot in the future,
a future threatened by
those old cold warriors
and their bankrupt philosophy:
trust no one,
eat or be eaten,
might means right.
This land is *my* land — and that is my land too.

Daughters do things differently.
They say no to war,
view violence as abject failure
and acquisition as the root of evil.
Compassion, caring, fairness,
mutual support, equitable
distribution of resources:
this is not a communist revolution,
just another page in human evolution.

Sacrificial Daughters

Agamemnon and my father
had this in common:
daughters sacrificed for gain,
to maintain order,
to assert authority,
to make a point.

Daughters who survive
disappear from view.

Orpheus and Eurydice

Sang Orpheus to Eurydice
when he took her for his wife:
"My beloved, my fair nymph,
I will love you all my life."

But one day he came home from work
to find a scene of disarray.
Nosey neighbors noticed that
Eurydice had not been seen
around or in the house.
Her cell phone went unanswered
though the car was parked outside.

A gruff detective in rumpled suit
took Orpheus aside and told him
that his lovely wife had died.
Bitten by a snake of the most venomous kind,
she was carried off by Hades
to a place no mortal beings would ever find.

Orpheus cried out "I must free my wife or die"
as he grabbed his lyre and headed out
to confront the lord of Hades in his lair.
Charmed by Orpheus's music
Hades let him seek his wife
and lead her home where
she could resume her life.

Only one condition did Hades demand:
that Orpheus resist the urge
to look back at Eurydice's ascent.
But as they began to climb the stairs,
he was overcome with desire
to see his beloved's face and hair,
and to ensure that she was there.

He turned and for the last time
saw that beautiful sweet face,
as she lost her footing and began to fall,
back into that sepulchral place.

Orpheus was inconsolable
for he had lost his much loved wife,
but he could not place the blame
on anyone but himself.
From that day he made a pledge
to play only sad sweet songs,
and to practice patience, without which,
his quest to save his poor wife
went so terribly wrong.

Orpheus

You only love once.
Only one pulls back the curtain.
Only once the curtain is pulled back.
The rest is planning, practice, training —
then mourning.

Like a cat caught in a snowstorm,
I seek directions to the afterlife.
Someone is waiting there for me.

Haiku: Eurydice

I'm here.
Don't look back.
Trust me.

Appendix: Early Poems 1971-1975

Van Gogh

When Vincent made a picture
the world remained the same
but every tortured brush stroke
made the man a bit less sane.

Sanity's a luxury
that only fools can buy:
old Vincent did without it
'cause the price was much too high.

Portrait of Mrs. Chagall, no. 2

Green faced lady with the purple dress —
she looks so calm, so lovely.
I'd like to get to know her but I can't:
she is just a picture hanging on the wall,
looking not at but somehow through me.
On her shoulder sits a red devil.
Overhead flies a blue bird.
In her lap Love sleeps.
Her face is green because she is hiding,
as the earth hides under grass.

Vanishing Point

Gone is like
it never happened
only
you know what
almost
but didn't
and now
is
gone.

Nocturne

The night
in all its sable mystery descends,
and the light
of a day that has died
clings to the crest of the hill
with all its might.
And see,
behind a fragile veil of leaves,
the moon is bright,
the stars come into sight.
How still,
how cold,
the silent tingling air
that covers all
and makes the leaves
to fall.

Solitude

Reading by the fire
on a cold and snowy day,
the Viking's lady sat alone,
the sleeping mastiff
by her side.
The Viking's lady sat alone.
The Viking's lady read alone.

"There are no heroes,
only men," the Viking's lady wept,
and as she turned the page
a teardrop fell
on the colorful vignette.
The Viking's lady wept alone.
The Viking's lady, left alone.

She closed the book
and put it down;
the dog barked at the noise.
"The snow has stopped,"
she murmured
as she stirred the dying fire.
The Viking's lady felt alone.
The Viking's lady was alone.

The Viking's lady smiled
and the sun
broke through the clouds
making golden, dancing patterns
on the floor around her gown.
The Viking's lady smiled alone.
The Viking's lady left, alone.

Song

Don't give me apples,
don't give me bread,
I'm living in a madhouse
and I don't know what I've said.

We've all had savoy truffle
and eaten all your lies:
just leave me here to daydream
until the day I die.

That cardboard Buddha's watching
as my head starts to scream.
I don't know where we're going
'cause things aren't what they seem.

Refrain:

*They tell me this is living, baby,
but I'm hoping that it's just a dream.*

I drive a used car,
drink the cheapest wine,
and yet when people ask me
I say I'm doing fine.

I went to fancy schools
and learned how sweet life could be,
but now I'm on the street
and no one's talking to me.

So keep your hard earned money,
I don't want your advice.
Your way may be more simple
but I can't afford the price.

Refrain:

They tell me this is living, baby,
but I'm hoping that it's just a dream.

Aberration

This small child with dark eyes
and straight brown hair
will someday paraphrase
eternity's original mistake.
Not, it must be stressed, in defiance
or in some facetious way;
not at odds with elemental forces
or repugnant to delicate taste;
but consistent with the fishy smell
of foggy nights in March,
and the boom, the groan, the trembling sound
of dinosaurs' rebirth.

The Fire

The lady turned, the dancers paused:
"Who comes," she cried, but no reply.
"Go on, my friends. It must have been
the wind I heard."

The dancers leaped like tongues of fire,
and in the loft a local choir
was making sounds for all to hear,
but nothing stilled the lady's fear.

The night was chill, but not a breeze
was stirring in the autumn leaves.
What was it then that called to her?
What bade her leave her cozy hearth?

The lady rose, the music ceased.
"Continue, friends, but without me."
And saying this, she left alone.

The great door gave at her soft touch,
and night things came to welcome her.
She smiled, "I knew it must be thus!"
as she ran into the thankless night.

But with her words the night sounds ceased
and in their place she then could hear
the tramp of hooves, the falling trees,
the labored breath of burning leaves.
She turned to run but could not move;
its strength was greater than her fear.

A fire destroyed the woods that night,
 and many came to see the sight.
They never found her body, but
 they placed a stone amidst the ruins.
"Here was," it said, "a lady lost
 to fire and dark—we fear she's dead."

Memory

Take each dream and mold it
like a little piece of clay.
Crush it.
Bend it.
Roll it.
Blend it.
Shape it as you like,
then flatten it out on the table,
and leave it there to dry.

Dreams are like clay,
and clay cannot become what it is not.
Flatten them out and they will dry
to a permanent reminder
of a moment's surrender.

Fragments: Unrequited Love

A car drives past my window,
a low light burns by the bed:
love is not a healthy state of mind.

    ***

dog bark blood red
on now love
soft step don't touch
try somehow
black brack nights pass
eyes light on
comes sleep while weep
tears run down
pillow-slip moist stain
alone again

    ***

Keep silent then —
the message in your eyes
is not enough.
I'm tired of eating dreams
of sleeping thoughts
and waking wishes.
Keep silent then
and we'll go on
as if we never knew
another way.

Wailing for Her Demon Lover

On a blue night in a dead town
Death's mistress wanders up and down
the bony labyrinth of rhyme.
In the sky a purple passage
leads a way through Flora's frigid horns.

A bell tolls in the tower
and a low lamp glows by a window
on a street where sleeplessness
lingers like an anxious mother
over the crib of her sick child.

On the surface of the stream
a street-light stutters,
and in the house this sane light
keeps night's creatures out of sight
while Death's sweet lady rocks her red dreams,
weaves her soft sighs into song.

After the First Death

Death-pale pained faces,
hiding from themselves,
lost in placid, mundane lives
they've not survived
the agony of being born
and so, upright,
they walk and talk:
the living dead.

They haunt me in my waking hours
with cheerful smiles:
flowers blooming in a vase,
cut from the source, they still retain
a bright facade of thriving life.

But we know:
we've looked into the water jar
and seen the steel-cut stems:
we'll not be fooled again
by such pretense.

Vermont Holiday

Snowflakes, like doves' thoughts,
fall so quietly
and make even the sound
of the chickadee feeding at the window
seem a great noise
by comparison.

A snowplow rumbles past,
leaving a wall of snow and gravel
up and down the road.
Soon all the snow is trodden,
packed, yellow, dirty.

The temperature rises, and the snow is slush.
The temperature falls, and the snow is ice.
The rains come, and the snow is gone.

White snow, and soft,
like the gentle thoughts of doves,
is not of this world.

Untitled

I remain in the glume after threshing;
my love emboldens me.
Embowered in this evergreen
your growing pains I feel:
cupidity is only just
the half of it.

About the Author...

Lucy Wilson is a professor of English at Loyola Marymount University in Los Angeles. She received her doctorate from Temple University. Her work in modern British, Caribbean and contemporary U.S. literature has appeared in several journals and anthologies, including *Modern Fiction Studies*, *Journal of Caribbean Studies*, and *Review of Contemporary Literature*. Her first book, *In Due Season: Essays on Novels of Development by Caribbean Women Writers*, was published by University Press of America in 2008. Lucy teaches modern literature and poetry writing. Her poems reflect her fifteen year struggle with Parkinson's Disease, her concern for the environment, and such transformational activities as yoga and acupuncture. Her first poetry collection, *Wind on Water: Poems on Healing Arts and Songs of Love*, was published by Transcendent Zero Press early in 2015. She was a feature performer at Holidays Shindig 2015 in Houston, Texas.

www.ingramcontent.com/pod-product-compliance
Lightning Source LLC
Chambersburg PA
CBHW051659090426
42736CB00013B/2448